Feb. 23, 2010

ALGONQUIN AREA PUBLIC LIBRARY DISTRICT

3 1488 00498 5438

D1207537

Isaac Newton:

Groundbreaking Physicist and Mathematician

J
921
NEW

by Jane Weir

Science Contributor
Sally Ride Science

Science Consultant
Michael E. Kopecky, Science Educator

Algonquin Area Public Library
2600 Harnish Drive
Algonquin, IL 60102

MISSION: SCIENCE

Developed with contributions from Sally Ride Science™

Sally Ride
Science

Sally Ride Science™ is an innovative content company dedicated to fueling young people's interests in science.

Our publications and programs provide opportunities for students and teachers to explore the captivating world of science—from astrobiology to zoology.

We bring science to life and show young people that science is creative, collaborative, fascinating, and fun.

To learn more, visit www.SallyRideScience.com

First hardcover edition published in 2009 by
Compass Point Books
151 Good Counsel Drive
P.O. Box 669
Mankato, MN 56002-0669

Editor: Robert McConnell
Designer: Heidi Thompson
Editorial Contributor: Sue Vander Hook

Art Director: LuAnn Ascheman-Adams
Creative Director: Joe Ewest
Editorial Director: Nick Healy
Managing Editor: Catherine Neitge

Copyright © 2010 Teacher Created Materials Publishing
Teacher Created Materials is a copyright owner of the content contained in this title.
Published in cooperation with Teacher Created Materials and Sally Ride Science.
Printed in the United States of America.

 This book was manufactured with paper containing at least 10 percent post-consumer waste.

Library of Congress Cataloging-in-Publication Data
Weir, Jane, 1976–
 Isaac Newton : groundbreaking physicist and mathematician / by Jane
Weir.—1st hardcover ed.
    p. cm.—(Mission: Science)
 Includes index.
 ISBN 978-0-7565-4229-0 (library binding)
 1. Newton, Isaac, Sir, 1642–1727—Juvenile literature.
 2. Physicists—Great Britain—Biography—Juvenile literature.
 3. Mathematicians—Great Britain—Biography—Juvenile literature.
 I.Title. II. Series.
 QC16.N7W335 2010
 530.092—dc22
 [B]   2009003674

Visit Compass Point Books on the Internet at *www.compasspointbooks.com*
or e-mail your request to *custserv@compasspointbooks.com*

Table of Contents

Imagine a world where nobody understands why the moon goes around Earth, or why Earth goes around the sun. Imagine that people don't know why things fall when they are dropped, or why things stay where they are placed.

This was the world before Isaac Newton, who was one of the greatest scientists and mathematicians of all time. Although many doubted his theories and criticized his ideas, Newton laid the foundation for an accurate understanding of gravity, other forces, and motion.

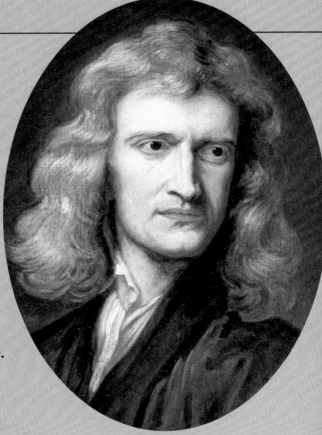

Isaac Newton is still honored for his monumental achievements.

A Christmas Baby

According to the calendar used in Newton's time, his birthday was December 25, 1642. But using today's calendar, his birthday was January 4, 1643.

He also created an important type of mathematics called calculus. It is still used by mathematicians, scientists, and engineers.

Isaac Newton was born December 25, 1642, in Woolsthorpe-by-Colsterworth, Lincolnshire, England. His father, who also was named Isaac Newton, was a sheep farmer. He died three months before young Isaac was born. Because Isaac was born too early, he was tiny and not expected to live.

When Isaac was 3 years old, his mother, Hannah, remarried. She went to live with her new husband, Barnabas Smith, who wouldn't let her bring Isaac along. He was left in the care of his mother's parents and seldom saw his mother for the next seven years. She had three more children with her new husband.

Newton grew up in the countryside.

Isaac attended neighborhood schools, where teachers reported that he was lazy and didn't pay attention. What he wrote showed sadness and anger, which might have resulted from his abandonment. When Barnabas Smith died, in 1653, Isaac's mother returned to Isaac. She brought along her three other children.

Two years later, at the age of 12, Isaac left home to attend King's School in Grantham. At that time many boys from well-off families went away to school. Isaac learned basic academic subjects, but not math, which wasn't taught. He found the lessons boring, however. So, on his own, he explored, experimented, and questioned how the world worked.

A Very Old School

King's School, which Newton attended from 1655 to 1660, has been educating boys for more than 500 years. It has grown a lot since Newton's time. Today the school has more than 950 students.

Did You Know?

The name "I. Newton" is carved on a window ledge at King's School. Isaac Newton is believed to have done the carving.

When Isaac was nearly 17, his mother made him leave King's School and return home. She wanted him to become a sheep farmer like his father. Isaac was not happy about her decision, and he did not do well as a farmer.

The next year, his mother sent him back to King's School. In a year, Isaac was ready for Trinity College, which was part of the University of Cambridge. Students at the university studied Aristotle, an ancient Greek philosopher. But Newton wanted to read about newer ideas. On his own, he studied the ideas of modern philosophers and scientists of his time, such as Descartes, Copernicus, and Galileo. Newton graduated from Cambridge in January 1665.

Legend says that seeing an apple fall made Newton think about how gravity works.

Newton had a fine record at King's School.

Newton used math to figure out what was happening in nature. In fact, he developed a new kind of math that he called a method of "fluxions." It was later called calculus. Newton didn't publish his mathematical methods until he had a final solution to a problem, which sometimes took many years.

Newton was particularly interested in motion and the natural forces, such as gravity, that cause objects to move or to stay in place. Newton didn't know what caused these forces, but he knew he could measure their effects.

He also studied light. With a triangle-shaped wedge of glass—a prism—Newton found that white light contains all the colors of the rainbow. He spent most of his life trying to explain natural events.

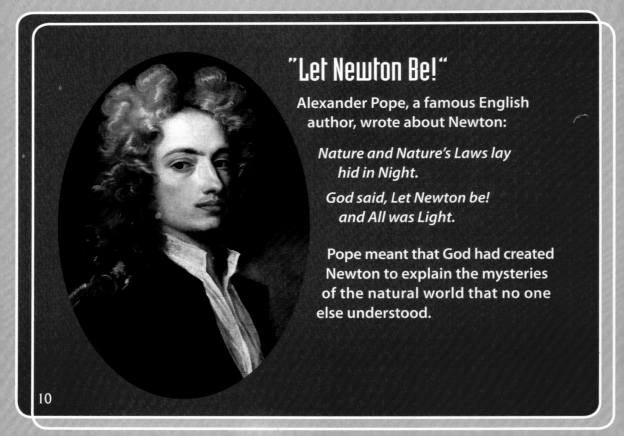

"Let Newton Be!"

Alexander Pope, a famous English author, wrote about Newton:

Nature and Nature's Laws lay hid in Night.

God said, Let Newton be! and All was Light.

Pope meant that God had created Newton to explain the mysteries of the natural world that no one else understood.

Laura Bassi
[1711–1778]

One of the first scientists to study and follow the teachings of Isaac Newton was Laura Bassi of Italy. She was also the first woman to teach physics at a European university.

Bassi taught courses on Newton's physics for 28 years, and she was the person who did the most to introduce Newton's ideas to Italy. During her years as a professor, Bassi was married and raised 12 children. She also fought to have more responsibilities at the university, better pay, and more advanced equipment for experiments.

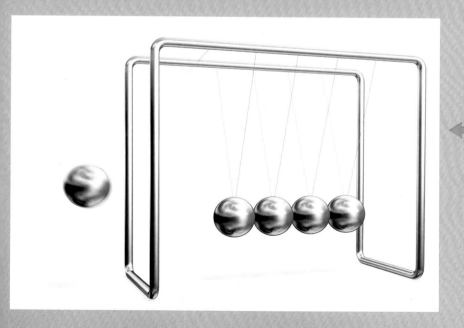

A toy called a Newton's cradle demonstrates some of Newton's laws.

The *Principia*

Newton went on to become a professor at Trinity College. He continued to study, experiment, and solve problems—often day and night. In 1672, at about the age of 30, Newton was invited to become a member of the Royal Society. The society was created to encourage learning and support scientific research.

Society members met and talked about things that puzzled them. Sometimes, if they couldn't solve a problem, they would give it to one another as a challenge. Newton was one of the best at solving mathematical problems.

In 1687 Newton published a three-volume set of books that described his theories. *Philosophiae Naturalis Principia Mathematica* (usually just called the *Principia*)

became one of the most important scientific works of all time. His work would bring him never-ending fame.

The *Principia*, with its complex mathematics, was difficult to understand. But, as one historian wrote, Newton showed that "simple laws explain

A Dark Force?

Philosophers in Newton's time criticized Newton's theory of gravity because he didn't explain what caused it. Gravity seemed like a mysterious, dark force, which frightened people. Newton didn't try to describe what gravity is; he just explained how gravity affects things.

The Newton

To honor Isaac Newton, the standard international unit used to measure force is called the newton.

complicated things." Newton presented the law of gravity, which showed why celestial bodies, such as planets, are attracted to each other. He explained how objects move in air and water. He also wrote about the motion of planets and other bodies in space.

Newtonian Mechanics

Newton described forces so well that the system used today to figure out how things move is named for him—Newtonian mechanics. Using Newton's math, you can map the path of a strawberry as it falls through the air into a bowl of cereal. You can also figure out how fast a stone will fall after it is dropped and how much effort is needed to pick up a book. We can describe the moon's path around Earth. In fact, the movement of everything we see can be explained with Newton's math.

The strawberries fall because of gravity, a natural force that Newton explained. The splashing of the milk shows one of his laws of motion.

Newton's Laws of Motion

Isaac Newton is probably most famous for his three laws of motion. The laws explain what happens when objects move—and when they don't move. He described his laws of motion in the *Principia*.

The First Law

Newton's first law of motion is also called the law of inertia. Inertia means resistance to a change in motion. In modern language, this law of motion says:

An object that is at rest or moving steadily in a straight line will stay that way until an outside force acts on it.

What Newton meant was that as long as a new force doesn't push or pull on an object, its state of motion won't change. Things that are still will stay still. Things moving at a constant speed in a straight line will keep

According to Newton's first law, a bicycle's motion won't change until some force, such as braking, makes it change.

doing that. Of course, there usually is at least one outside force—the downward pull of gravity. So an arrow shot from a bow falls to the ground instead of going straight out into space.

The Second Law

Newton's second law of motion is often called the law of acceleration. It says:

A change in an object's motion depends on the amount of force applied to it, the direction in which the force moves, and the mass of the object.

This law describes what happens when something pushes or pulls an object. The stronger the force, the faster the object will speed up or slow down. A stronger force is needed to make a heavier object speed up or slow down. For example, it is easier to stop a bicycle than a car. This law also says that an object will move in the direction in which the force is going.

Pushing an adult on a swing takes more force than pushing a child.

Newton wrote a lot about science and other topics, such as religion.

The Third Law

Newton's third law of motion is the law of action and reaction. This law says:

For every action, there is an equal and opposite reaction.

Newton explained that when a force pushes on an object, the object pushes back in the opposite direction. The force of the pushing back is called the reaction force.

This law explains why we can move a rowboat in water. The water pushes back on the oar as much as the oar pushes on the water, which moves the boat. The law also explains why the pull of gravity doesn't make a chair crash through the floor—the floor pushes back enough to offset gravity. When you hit a baseball, the bat pushes on the ball, but the ball also pushes on the bat.

Baseball hitters take advantage of the third law of motion.

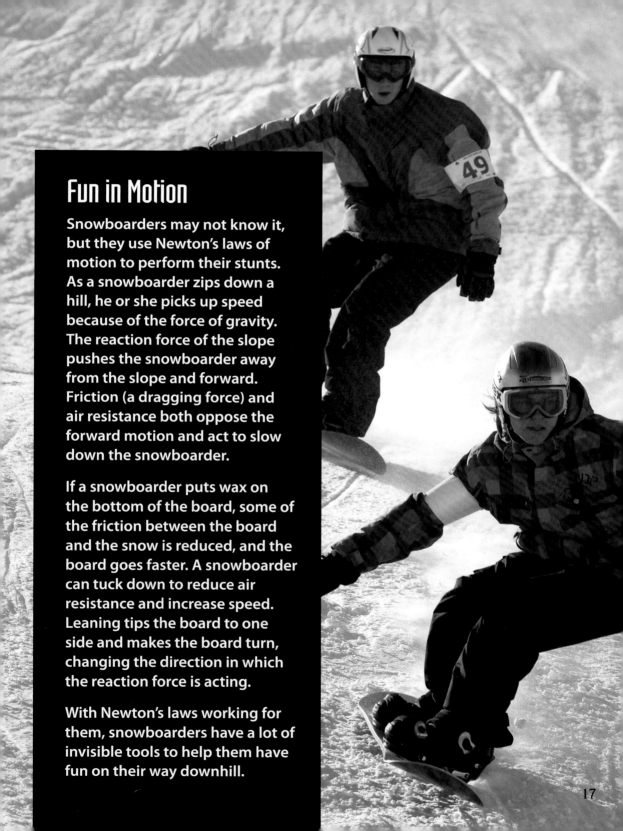

Fun in Motion

Snowboarders may not know it, but they use Newton's laws of motion to perform their stunts. As a snowboarder zips down a hill, he or she picks up speed because of the force of gravity. The reaction force of the slope pushes the snowboarder away from the slope and forward. Friction (a dragging force) and air resistance both oppose the forward motion and act to slow down the snowboarder.

If a snowboarder puts wax on the bottom of the board, some of the friction between the board and the snow is reduced, and the board goes faster. A snowboarder can tuck down to reduce air resistance and increase speed. Leaning tips the board to one side and makes the board turn, changing the direction in which the reaction force is acting.

With Newton's laws working for them, snowboarders have a lot of invisible tools to help them have fun on their way downhill.

17

Gravity

Isaac Newton was the first person to show that the force that makes planets go around the sun is the same force that makes things fall to Earth.

According to a legend, Newton figured out gravity when he saw an apple fall from a tree. He realized that gravity attracted both the apple and the moon to Earth. This legend is probably not true, but Newton did learn how gravity works when he was spending time in the countryside.

Gravity is what holds us on the ground and keeps us from floating into space. It also keeps Earth going around the sun and the moon going around Earth. Without gravity the universe couldn't stay together. So gravity is probably the most important force of all.

By watching the planets in the sky, Newton figured out that the planets were being pulled toward the sun. The closer the planets were to the sun, the stronger the pull.

Escape From Earth

If you make something go fast enough, it will have enough force to escape Earth's gravity and go into orbit. This is called escape velocity—the speed needed to overcome the pull of gravity. On the surface of Earth, escape velocity is almost 7 miles (11.2 kilometers) per second, which is about 10 times as fast as a speeding bullet. Reaching escape velocity using powerful rocket engines is how space vehicles can leave Earth.

Emilie de Breteuil
[1706—1749]

French mathematician and physicist Emilie de Breteuil was a follower of Newton's teachings. Born into a wealthy family, she received a good education, unlike most girls of her time. After she married and had three children, she began to study the work of Newton.

De Breteuil's greatest achievement was probably translating Newton's *Principia* into French, which made his work well known in her country. The text included her comments and theories. Her translation is still used today.

Gravity keeps the planets in their orbits around the sun.

Newton also observed the moon and concluded that it was being pulled toward Earth. He understood that if Earth's gravity ever stopped pulling on it, the moon would move away from Earth in a straight line. The force of Earth's gravity on the moon pulls it around the Earth in a circle.

Imagine a ball on the end of a string. If you swing the ball around your head, the tension in the string acts like gravity. It keeps the ball moving in a circle. If you let go of the string, the ball flies off. That's what the moon would do without Earth's gravity.

Why doesn't Earth's gravity pull the moon all the way down to Earth? Because the moon has energy from its own motion. If some huge force stopped the moon from moving, it would lose that energy and fall to Earth.

An experiment with a post, string, and ball can show how gravity keeps the moon from moving away from Earth.

moon

Earth

20

Why Does a Roller Coaster Make Your Stomach Feel Funny?

When you jump off something high or go down a steep slope on a roller coaster, you can tell that gravity is working on you. You feel weightless when this happens because there is no reaction force pressing up under you. On a roller coaster ride, gravity makes you and your seat accelerate downward at the same speed. What's inside your body also moves down, but since your body is mostly water, there is more resistance there than on the outside. That stops some of your internal organs from accelerating as fast as the outside of your body. First you feel a jolt, as if your stomach were coming up into your mouth. Then your insides catch up with the outside of your body. Everything accelerates together, and you feel normal—until the roller coaster reaches the next slope.

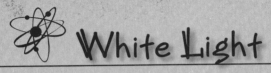

White Light

Isaac Newton also made important discoveries about light. Scientists then believed that white light was natural light and that colored light was light that had changed after going through air or water. They thought a rainbow—a display of all the colors, called a spectrum—came from some kind of prism, which changed the light.

passed through the prism. What Newton learned helped to explain how rainbows form.

Newton changed scientists' understanding of light, but many people criticized his ideas. He got so tired of defending them that he didn't publish what he had learned about light until 30 years after he completed it.

Newton did an experiment with two glass prisms. He discovered that if the spectrum coming from one prism was put through another prism, the colors didn't change again. From this he knew that white light was made of all the colors of the rainbow. It was just broken into separate colors when it

White light is a combination of all colors. A prism separates the colors and makes all of them visible.

Building on the Past

Isaac Newton wrote that if he could see farther than other people, it was because he had stood "upon the shoulders of giants." He meant that his discoveries had their roots in the ideas of scientists who had experimented and made discoveries before him. That's true of many scientific discoveries— they are built on the work that other scientists have done. Future scientists will use today's discoveries to learn even more.

Isaac Newton was not just a physicist and mathematician, but also an inventor. Some of his inventions are still used today, such as the reflector telescope, which uses mirrors. That made it much better than the eyeglass-type curved lenses that had been used in telescopes. Newton's telescope is particularly good for looking at groups of stars.

High-quality lenses were important to Newton. He did an experiment that showed him that shining a light on a lens and a glass plate at a certain angle produced rings of light. These rings, which came to be called Newton's rings, are still used to test the quality of lens surfaces.

Newton created a formula—called the lens equation—to describe how far away a lens can focus light. His formula is used in making telescopes, microscopes, reading glasses, and anything else with a lens.

Newton was the first scientist to describe the main idea of a sextant. When this instrument was built, many years later, sailors could use it to find where they were at sea, based on the locations of the sun and stars.

Newton's Laws for Chickens

Newton was such a famous and important scientist that people sometimes tell jokes about him. Here's a well-known joke about Newton's laws of motion and gravity.

Why did the chicken cross the road?

First law of motion: Chickens at rest tend to stay at rest. Chickens in motion tend to cross the road.

Second law of motion: The chicken was pushed.

Third law of motion: The chicken was pushed by another chicken that knocked itself over by pushing so hard.

Law of gravity: The chicken was attracted to a bigger chicken waiting across the road.

Master Problem Solver

In 1696 Newton was put in charge of the Royal Mint, which made British coins. His job was to replace old handmade coins with new ones made by machines. He was also supposed to find people who made fake money.

In honor of Newton's service at the mint, Queen Anne of England made him a knight. That gave him a title: Sir Isaac Newton.

Newton was still interested in science and mathematics, though. In 1703 he had become president of the Royal Society, which promoted excellence in scientific research. And he never had stopped solving difficult mathematical problems. When a Swiss mathematician presented a problem for all the mathematicians of Europe to solve, Newton took on the challenge. Although

Newton was president of the Royal Society until he died.

in his life, perhaps because criticism made him angry.

Isaac Newton died March 20, 1727, at the age of 84. He was buried at Westminster Abbey in London, where many important English people are buried. Newton's ideas and laws, however, were not laid to rest with him.

For hundreds of years, his ideas have influenced almost every area of science. His findings have led to advancements in medicine, chemistry, rocket science, computers, and other fields. Great inventors have relied on Newton's laws to develop machines and technology that work with precision.

Newton is a towering figure in the history of ideas.

the mathematicians were allowed six months to solve it, Newton came up with the answer in one night.

But Newton didn't like explaining how he solved a problem, so he published his answer without giving his name in a Royal Society magazine. Newton was secretive about many things

The world is indebted to Isaac Newton—a scientific and mathematical genius. He gave the world valuable information and changed forever the way people view science and mathematics.

Sally Ride
Science

Civil Engineer: Oksana Wall

Walt Disney World

Riding High

When Oksana Wall was 13, she and her family came from Venezuela to visit Walt Disney World in Orlando, Florida. She wondered who created the rides.

When she found out they were designed by engineers, she decided she wanted to become an engineer, too—and work for Disney, of course. After earning a master's degree in civil engineering from the Florida Institute of Technology, she reached her goal—she did indeed go to work for Disney.

When Wall designs rides, she uses Newton's law of gravity and his three laws of motion. Knowing how forces make things move helps her create rides for Disney that are safe and unique. "I really love working on many projects," she says. "I have a blast at my job."

What is the best part of Wall's job? "We get to enjoy the attractions ourselves," she said, "and we get to see our guests enjoy them, too."

On the Team

Designing an amusement park ride isn't a one-person job. It requires teamwork. A lot of people—mechanical engineers, electrical engineers, architects, and artists—have to work together and cooperate with one another to make the best possible ride.

A Job for You?

Civil engineers help to design buildings and other structures that many people use every day. If you were a civil engineer, you might …

• construct stadiums or skyscrapers

• plan highways or airports

• design bridges or dams

Name:	Isaac Newton
Date of birth:	December 25, 1642
Nationality:	English
Birthplace:	Woolsthorpe-by-Colsterworth, Lincolnshire, England
Parents:	Isaac Newton (1606–1642) Hannah Ayscough Newton Smith (?–1679) Barnabas Smith (stepfather) (1582–1653)
Siblings:	Mary Smith Pilkington (half sister) (1647–?) Benjamin Smith (half brother) (1651–?) Hannah Smith Barton (half sister) (1652–?)
Date of death:	March 20, 1727
Place of burial:	Westminster Abbey, London
Field of study:	Physics, mathematics
Contributions to science:	Newton's laws of motion, law of universal gravitation, calculus
Awards and honors:	President of the Royal Society, knighted by Queen Anne

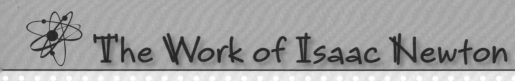
1642	Isaac Newton is born December 25 in Woolsthorpe-by-Colsterworth in Lincolnshire, England
1646	Father dies; mother marries again and moves away, leaving Isaac with grandparents
1653	Mother returns with three of Isaac's half siblings
1655	Attends King's School in Grantham
1659	Called home to learn farming
1661	Attends Trinity College at University of Cambridge
1665	Graduates from Cambridge; begins research on gravity, calculus, and optics
1668	Earns a master's degree from Cambridge
1669	Becomes professor of mathematics at Cambridge
1672	Becomes member of the Royal Society
1679	Mother dies
1684	Work on calculus is published
1687	*Principia* is published
1696	Put in charge of the Royal Mint
1703	Becomes president of the Royal Society
1705	Knighted by Queen Anne
1727	Dies March 20; buried in Westminster Abbey in London, England

Glossary

acceleration—rate of increase of speed

calculus—branch of mathematics that deals with the measurement of changing quantities

escape velocity—minimum speed needed to escape a gravitational field

force—factor, such as pushing or pulling, that causes an object to move or change speed or direction

friction—force that resists an object's motion

gravity—force of attraction between objects, such as Earth's downward pull

inertia—tendency of an object to remain at rest or in motion unless acted upon by an outside force

physicist—scientist who studies physics

physics—science that studies matter, energy, force, and motion

prism—solid clear glass object, usually in a triangular shape, that splits a beam of white light into all colors

reflecting microscope—device that uses mirrors instead of lenses to magnify very small things

reflector telescope—device that uses mirrors instead of lenses to look at distant objects, such as stars

sextant—measuring device used by sailors to find their position using the sun or stars

spectrum—distribution of colors produced when white light is split by a prism

white light—light that appears colorless but is made of all the colors of the spectrum

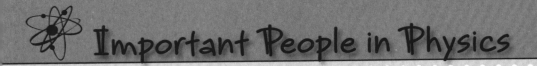

André Marie Ampère (1775–1836)
French physicist and mathematician who determined that electric currents produce magnetic fields; current strength is measured in amperes in his honor

Antoine Henri Becquerel (1852–1908)
French physicist who discovered radioactivity by accident in 1896 when a piece of uranium made an image on a photographic plate; unit for measuring radioactivity, the becquerel, is named for him; won the Nobel Prize for physics in 1903, along with Pierre and Marie Curie

Niels Bohr (1885–1962)
Danish physicist who received the Nobel Prize in physics in 1922 for his contribution to the discovery that atoms are made of protons, neutrons, and electrons

Max Born (1882–1970)
German physicist who won the Nobel Prize in physics in 1954 and helped to develop quantum mechanics, a branch of physics that deals with the structure and behavior of atoms and smaller particles

Pierre Curie (1859–1906)
French physicist who shared the 1903 Nobel Prize in physics with his wife, Marie Curie, and Antoine Becquerel in 1903 for their research on radiation

Marie Sklodowska Curie (1867–1934)
Polish-French physicist and chemist who was awarded two Nobel Prizes (1903 and 1911) for her pioneering work in radioactivity

John Dalton (1766–1844)
English chemist and physicist who developed the atomic theory of matter

Albert Einstein (1879–1955)
German-born American theoretical physicist and one of the greatest scientists in history; best known for his theories of relativity, especially one describing the relationship between mass and energy using the formula $E = mc^2$; won the Nobel Prize in physics in 1921

Michael Faraday (1791–1867)
English physicist and chemist who proposed the idea of magnetic lines of force, developed the first electrical generator, and pioneered the study of low temperatures

Maria Göppert-Mayer (1906–1972)
American physicist known for her research on the nucleus of atoms; received the Nobel Prize for physics in 1963, becoming the second woman to receive the award (Marie Curie was the first)

Werner Heisenberg (1901–1976)
German physicist who developed the uncertainty principle, which advanced modern physics; also determined that the atomic nucleus consists of protons and neutrons; won the Nobel Prize in physics in 1932

Irène Joliot-Curie (1897–1956)
French chemist and daughter of Marie and Pierre Curie; with her husband, Frédéric Joliot, she received the Nobel Prize for chemistry in 1935 for discovering artificial radioactivity

James Prescott Joule (1818–1889)
English physicist who helped to show that energy is
not lost or gained when it changes form; basic unit of
thermal energy is called the joule in his honor

Gottfried Wilhelm Leibniz (1646–1716)
German mathematician who developed calculus
independently of Isaac Newton

Ernst Mach (1838–1916)
Austrian physicist who discovered that airflow is
disturbed at the speed of sound; mach numbers, which
show how fast something is moving compared with the
speed of sound, were named for him

James Clerk Maxwell (1831–1879)
British physicist whose math equations were a basis for
understanding electromagnetism; determined that light
is electromagnetic radiation

Dimitri Ivanovich Mendeleev (1834–1907)
Russian chemist who created the first version of the
periodic table of the elements

Albert A. Michelson (1852–1931)
American physicist who showed that the speed of light
is constant; his work laid the foundation for Albert
Einstein's theories of relativity; in 1907 he became the
first American to win a Nobel Prize in science when he
received the Nobel Prize in physics

Edward Morley (1838–1923)
American chemist and physicist who, with Albert Michelson, developed the interferometer to show that the velocity of light is a constant

J. Robert Oppenheimer (1904–1967)
American physicist who worked in astrophysics and directed the Manhattan Project, a U.S. government program that created the first atomic bomb

Max Planck (1858–1947)
German theoretical physicist who developed the quantum theory to explain the behavior of radiant energy; won the Nobel Prize in physics in 1918

Wilhelm Conrad Röntgen (1845–1923)
German physicist who discovered X-rays in 1895; won the first Nobel Prize in physics in 1901

Ernest Rutherford (1871–1937)
English physicist who studied the element uranium and became known as the father of nuclear physics

Joseph John Thomson (1856–1940)
English physicist who discovered the electron and separated isotopes of chemical elements; received the Nobel Prize in physics in 1906

Additional Resources

Boerst, William J. *Isaac Newton: Organizing the Universe*. Greensboro, N.C.: Morgan Reynolds Publishing, 2004.

Burnett, Betty. *The Laws of Motion: Understanding Uniform and Accelerated Motion*. New York: Rosen Publishing Group, 2005.

Krull, Kathleen. *Isaac Newton*. New York: Viking, 2006.

Nardo, Don. *Kinetic Energy: The Energy of Motion*. Minneapolis: Compass Point Books, 2008.

Riley, Peter D. *Forces and Movement*. North Mankato, Minn.: Smart Apple Media, 2006.

Rosinsky, Natalie M. *Sir Isaac Newton: Brilliant Mathematician and Scientist*. Minneapolis: Compass Point Books, 2008.

Internet Sites

FactHound offers a safe, fun way to find Internet sites related to this book. All of the sites on FactHound have been researched by our staff.

Here's all you do:
   Visit *www.facthound.com*
FactHound will fetch the best sites for you!

Index

About the Author

Jane Weir

Jane Weir grew up in Leicester, England. She graduated from the University of Sheffield with a master's degree in physics and astronomy, but gained much of her practical knowledge of physics through rock climbing. Weir lives in Salisbury, England, where she works as a scientist for the British government.

Image Credits

The Granger Collection, New York, cover (left), 7, 9, 10, 15 (right), 19 (top), 23, 26, 27, 30; pulsar75/Shutterstock, cover (right); Getty Images, 2; Vasile Tiplea/Shutterstock, 3, 21; Christie's Images/SuperStock, 6 (top); Mary Evans Picture Library/Alamy, 6 (bottom); Elmtree Images/Alamy, 8; Library of Congress, 11 (top); ErickN/Shutterstock, 11 (bottom); Diego Cervo/Shutterstock, 13; Photos.com, 14, 15 (left), 24 (middle); Pete Hoffman/Shutterstock, 16; Maxim Petrichuk/Shutterstock, 17; Jan Kaliciak/Shutterstock, 18; Jurgen Ziewe/Shutterstock, 19 (bottom); Peter Baxter/Shutterstock, 20; Jeff Daniels/Shutterstock, 22; Photo Researchers, Inc., 24 (left & right); Tim Bradley, 25 (all); Walt Disney World, 28; Michael Braun/iStockphoto, 29.